W9-BDE-270

SandCastle

Word Families Set 5

-op as in top

Amanda Rondeau

Consulting Editor Monica Marx, M.A./Reading Specialist

ABDO
Publishing Company

Published by SandCastle™, an imprint of ABDO Publishing Company, 4940 Viking Drive, Edina, Minnesota 55435.

Printed in the United States.

Credits
Edited by: Pam Price
Curriculum Coordinator: Nancy Tuminelly
Cover and Interior Design and Production: Mighty Media
Photo Credits: BananaStock Ltd., Brand X Pictures, Comstock, Corbis Images, Eyewire Images, PhotoDisc, Rubberball Productions, Stockbyte

Library of Congress Cataloging-in-Publication Data

Rondeau, Amanda, 1974-
        -Op as in top / Amanda Rondeau.
            p. cm. -- (Word families. Set V)
        Summary: Introduces, in brief text and illustrations, the use of the letter combination "op" in such words as "top," "chop," "prop," and "raindrop."
        ISBN 1-59197-252-3
        1. Readers (Primary) [1. Vocabulary. 2. Reading.] I. Title.

PE1119 .R696 2003
428.1--dc21   2002038215

SandCastle™ books are created by a professional team of educators, reading specialists, and content developers around five essential components that include phonemic awareness, phonics, vocabulary, text comprehension, and fluency. All books are written, reviewed, and leveled for guided reading, early intervention reading, and Accelerated Reader® programs and designed for use in shared, guided, and independent reading and writing activities to support a balanced approach to literacy instruction.

Let Us Know

After reading the book, SandCastle would like you to tell us your stories about reading. What is your favorite page? Was there something hard that you needed help with? Share the ups and downs of learning to read. We want to hear from you! To get posted on the ABDO Publishing Company Web site, send us e-mail at:

sandcastle@abdopub.com

SandCastle Level: Transitional

-op Words

cop

hop

lollipop

raindrop

stop

top

The cop helps Marty
cross the street.

The rabbit has to hop
across the snow.

Mike and Jane have
a big lollipop.

The splash was made
by a raindrop.

Will's dad taught him
how to stop.

Nick is at the top of the hill.

The Top
of the Crop

The cop grows flowers
as a crop.

The crop grows tall

and starts to flop.

The cop doesn't want
the crop to flop.

The cop makes
the flopping
stop.

She tries to prop up the crop
with a mop.

All this flopping
needs to stop!

The cop decides to chop
each floppy top.

She takes the crop
to the shop.

She sells each top
for a penny a pop!

When every top has
been sold,

it's time to shop!

The -op Word Family

chop	plop
cop	pop
crop	prop
drop	raindrop
flop	shop
hop	slop
lollipop	stop
mop	top

Glossary

Some of the words in this list may have more
than one meaning. The meaning listed here
reflects the way the word is used in the book.

across   from one side to the other

crop   a plant grown and
harvested for profit

flower   the part of a plant that
makes the fruit or seed

raindrop   a water drop that falls
from a cloud

street   road

About SandCastle™

A professional team of educators, reading specialists, and content developers created the SandCastle™ series to support young readers as they develop reading skills and strategies and increase their general knowledge. The SandCastle™ series has four levels that correspond to early literacy development in young children. The levels are provided to help teachers and parents select the appropriate books for young readers.

Emerging Readers
(no flags)

Beginning Readers
(1 flag)

Transitional Readers
(2 flags)

Fluent Readers
(3 flags)

These levels are meant only as a guide. All levels are subject to change.

ABDO
Publishing Company

To see a complete list of SandCastle™ books and other nonfiction titles from ABDO Publishing Company, visit www.abdopub.com or contact us at:

4940 Viking Drive, Edina, Minnesota 55435 • 1-800-800-1312 • fax: 1-952-831-1632